THE WORLD OF MARTIAL ARTS
SAMURAI

BY JIM OLLHOFF

Visit us at
www.abdopublishing.com

Editor: John Hamilton
Graphic Design: John Hamilton
Cover Design: Neil Klinepier
Cover Illustration: Getty Images
Interior Photos and Illustrations: p 1 samurai holding naginata, Getty Images; p 5 two samurai in battle, Getty Images; p 7 two samurai reenactors fighting, iStockphoto; p 8 samurai archer, Kabori Yasuo; p 9 two samurai with flags, Getty Images; p 10 samurai in boats, Mary Evans Picture Library; p 11 (top) Toyotomi Hideyoshi, unknown; p 11 (middle) section of globe showing Asia, iStockphoto; p 11 (bottom) map of Japan, Getty Images; p 12 scene from *Seven Samurai*, courtesy Toho Company; p 13 three samurai holding weapons, Getty Images; p 15 samurai kneeling, holding out sword, Getty Images; p 17 archer riding horse, Getty Images; p 18 woman using sword, Getty Images; p 19 samurai in official clothing, Getty Images; p 20 samurai kneeling, with two geishas, Getty Images; p 21 dish of rice, iStockphoto; p 22 samurai in armor holding sword, Getty Images; p 23 helmet with deer antlers, Getty Images; p 24 katana, iStockphoto; p 25 helmet, wakizashi, katana, Getty Images; p 27 full suit of armor, Getty Images; p 29 samurai with sword, Getty Images; p 31 kendo competitors, iStockphoto.

Library of Congress Cataloging-in-Publication Data

Ollhoff, Jim, 1959-
   Samurai / Jim Ollhoff.
      p. cm. -- (The world of martial arts)
   Includes index.
   ISBN 978-1-59928-983-0
   1. Samurai--Juvenile literature. I. Title.

DS827.S3O44 2008
952'.02--dc22
                        2007030553

武道

CONTENTS

THE SAMURAI

They were some of the most feared and respected warriors in all of history. They were legendary for their skill in battle and the honor with which they carried themselves. They were the *samurai*.

The samurai were warriors in medieval Japan. While their origins in Japan began as early as 200 A.D., the peak of their influence was from about 1200 A.D. to 1650 A.D. They were expert fighters, with an unsurpassed knowledge of martial arts. They knew how to use the bow and arrow, and the spear, but they were most famous for the use of the samurai sword.

The samurai swore an oath of loyalty to their leader, and would fight to the death to protect him or her. This oath made the samurai even more fearsome on the battlefield, because the samurai were not afraid of death.

The samurai were much more than martial arts experts. They also trained themselves in gentler arts as well. They studied philosophy, wrote poetry, and were often devout Buddhists. The samurai code of honor affected every part of their lives.

The samurai no longer exist. But even today, they capture our imagination with their skill, their loyalty, and their fearlessness.

Facing page: Two samurai warriors fight with swords during a battle in medieval Japan.

ORIGIN OF THE SAMURAI

For most of history, there was not a central government in Japan. Instead, there were local warlords who ruled small areas. Most tried to gain power and influence. Some simply wanted to protect themselves. Much of this fighting was among different clans, or family groups. One clan would go to war against another clan to gain control of farmland or other resources.

Some of the first recorded battles were under Queen Himiko (sometimes written as "Pimiko"). She tried to unite 28 clans into a single confederation. She had brief success by about 200 A.D., but the shaky peace quickly broke down.

Since the fighting was so frequent, clan leaders learned that giving swords to local farmers and asking them to fight was not a good way to defend the land. It was better to fight with a few professional warriors than a lot of farmers. Therefore, professional warriors began to emerge. These men practiced martial arts and became experts with weapons. By 800 A.D., local warlords and chieftains were relying on their own permanent warriors. These warriors were the military servants of the local chieftains. By about 900 A.D., the term "samurai" was used. The word means, "One who serves." The samurai served their local chieftain.

THE GEMPEI WAR

One of the most famous conflicts in Japanese history is the Gempei War, from 1180 to 1185 A.D. This series of battles was fought between two large clans, the Taira clan and the Minamoto clan. The battles were fought all over Japan and finally resulted in victory for the Minamoto clan. During this war, the samurai demonstrated how important they were to victory. The samurai were experts at archery and hand-to-hand combat, and showed little fear of death. This was the beginning of the age of the samurai.

Below: Two men dressed as samurai at a battle reenactment in Japan.

Above: During the Gempei War, a Minamoto clan archer called Nasu no Yoichi accepted a challenge from the Taira clan to shoot a small fan hundreds of feet away. Nasu no Yoichi struck the center of the fan. Both sides cheered his skill.

A story from the Gempei War illustrates life as a samurai. Toward the end of the war, after a battle in a valley called Ichi-no-Tani, the Taira army fled from the Minamoto samurai. The Taira warriors made it to their boats and sailed offshore, out of range of the Minamoto archers.

From the safety of their boats, the Taira clan made a challenge. They placed a tall pole with a fan on top at the bow of one of their boats and challenged the Minamoto archers to hit it. The Minamoto knew if they hit the fan with an arrow, it would embarrass the Taira. If they missed the fan, they would embarrass themselves.

The Minamoto's best archer, Nasu no Yoichi, approached the shore. Both sides held their breath, wondering if the archer could hit the fan. Nasu no Yoichi took aim, shot his arrow, and struck the fan in the center, sending it fluttering down. A cheer went up from both armies, saluting the ability of the Minamoto marksman. This was life as a samurai: often violent and bloody, but also filled with respect and honor for the skills of both friends and enemies.

The Gempei War started the legend of the samurai. However, that legend was cemented a few years later, during the battles against Kublai Khan and the Mongols.

THE MONGOL INVASION

By 1206 A.D., Genghis Khan had created the Mongolian Empire, which stretched all the way from China into Europe.

The ruler's grandson, Kublai Khan, wanted to invade Japan. In 1268, he sent ambassadors to Japan, asking for tribute. "Tribute" meant high taxes. Japan refused to pay, so Kublai Khan made plans to invade with 800 ships and 30,000 warriors.

Above: Two samurai reenactors at a festival in Japan.

In 1274, Kublai Khan sent his fleet toward Japan, but before his army could conquer the main island, a terrible storm arose, possibly a typhoon, sinking many ships and forcing the remainder of the ships back to the mainland.

Kublai Khan still wanted to attack Japan, so he sent ambassadors again, demanding tribute. This time, the Japanese officials killed the Mongol ambassadors. Kublai Khan was furious. The samurai knew he would attack again, and so they began to make defense plans.

This time, Kublai Khan wanted to attack with 200,000 men in 4,000 ships. He wanted no problems this time. Khan wanted to completely overwhelm the Japanese. However, in his impatience to attack, Kublai Khan made some serious errors. He needed so many boats that he didn't care where he got them. Unwisely, he used riverboats. These boats were fine for calm inland rivers, but they were very unstable on the ocean. Secondly, he used Chinese shipbuilders as slave labor. The Chinese were excellent shipbuilders, but Kublai Khan had just conquered them. Naturally, the Chinese were very resentful toward the Mongols. So, as they built the ships, they sabotaged many of them, making the ships unstable in bad weather.

Above: Japanese samurai defeat Kublai Khan's Mongol invaders in 1281.

In 1281, Kublai Khan and his 4,000 ships set sail for Japan. The samurai had built effective defenses on the shores, so the Mongols were not able to land a large fleet. Small Japanese ships darted between the large Mongol ships, causing havoc. When a Mongol ship did land, the Mongol soldiers were no match for the samurai in hand-to-hand fighting. To make matters worse, it was the middle of summer, and the food supply on the Mongol ships spoiled rapidly.

Still, despite the Mongol difficulty, everyone knew what the outcome would be. Eventually, the Mongols would land in force and get a foothold. Then, the enormous Mongol army would flood the few samurai on the shore.

However, before the Mongols could land in force, a storm came up. Many of the Mongol ships were unstable in the ocean. The Chinese had sabotaged many other boats. More than two-thirds of the Mongol ships were overturned by strong winds. A few Mongol ships limped back to the mainland. Japanese leaders believed this event was an intervention by the gods. They called the wind *kama-kazi*, or "divine wind." The Japanese leaders didn't know the Chinese had sabotaged the ships. They didn't realize that Kublai Khan had used riverboats. The Japanese leaders believed that the gods were with the samurai. The samurai were now the most respected class of people in Japan.

The Unification of Japan

The samurai continued to work for their chieftains for the next few generations. In the late 1500s, a man named Oda Nobunaga and one of his samurai, Toyotomi Hideyoshi, unified the country under one rule. For the first time in Japanese history, there was a single government. In 1588, Hideyoshi, now the country's shogun, or ruler, made it illegal for farmers and merchants to carry swords. Only the samurai could carry swords.

A few years later, the government passed a law making it illegal for samurai to farm the land. Even when there was no fighting, the samurai were not allowed to have any other job. Hideyoshi also made a law that only children of samurai could become samurai. Children not born into a samurai family could never become samurai. This period was the peak of samurai power and influence.

Above: Toyotomi Hideyoshi.

Bushido: Code of the Samurai

Samurai lived by a code of conduct called *bushido*, or "the way of the warrior." The most important part of the bushido code was allegiance to a master, or lord. The samurai swore an oath of loyalty, and would defend their lord until death. They followed their master's wishes, even if the master was making a wrong decision.

Samurai had a particular way of looking at their fleeting lives. They believed the purpose of life was to act honorably, without lying, cheating, or stealing. It meant to live by their word with honesty and integrity.

According to the bushido code, to act with honor is a worthy life, no matter how short. Samurai often used an example of how life is like a cherry blossom. A cherry blossom blooms in beautiful splendor, but then fades quickly. The samurai compared their lives to cherry blossoms. Life is beautiful, but only for a short time.

Since samurai knew they could die in the next battle, they thought a lot about death. They meditated about death and wrote poetry about it. They did this so that they wouldn't be afraid to die in battle. They believed that death was simply a part of the natural order of life. The most important thing in life was to live honorably.

Below: A scene from Japanese director Akira Kurosawa's *Seven Samurai.*

Above: Three samurai warriors, photographed in approximately 1880, holding various weapons of war, including a spear, bow, and naginata, a spear-like weapon with a curved blade at the end.

A samurai could bring honor to himself if he successfully defended his master. A samurai was honorable if he conducted his business dealings without cheating. If all his interactions with people were friendly and helpful, it was honorable. However, if he cheated, stole, or lied, a samurai would be dishonored. To indulge in harmful behaviors, to neglect duties, or to become too attached to material things would be dishonorable. If he failed at defending his master, he would be dishonored.

When a samurai was dishonored, it would bring shame upon him. This shame was so terrible that a samurai believed the way to bring back honor was to commit ritual suicide, or *seppuku*. In seppuku, sometimes called *hara-kiri*, a shamed samurai would thrust a sword into his own abdomen.

Some samurai, of course, did not follow the code. Many dishonored samurai did not commit seppuku. They simply left town. Many samurai abused their privileged status. Many believed that human life was cheap, that they could take any life they wanted. Many samurai wandered the countryside without a master. The Japanese called them *ronin*, or "masterless samurai." These ronin roamed the land looking for work, or looking for a fight.

Above: Samurai who were disgraced in battle or faced some other deep dishonor often committed *seppuku*, or ritual suicide.

Samurai Daily Life

Training

Training was very important for the samurai. They knew that good training might save their lives, or the lives of their masters. Young samurai often trained with wooden swords, since the razor-sharp samurai swords were too dangerous to give to unskilled students. As students improved, their teachers gave them edgeless swords that were completely blunt. Finally, between the ages of 13 and 16, families presented teenagers with their own samurai swords. This was a solemn ritual, where the boys also received their first haircuts. They were expected to keep their ponytails, the sign of a samurai, for the rest of their lives. To cut off their ponytails would be a terrible disgrace.

Days for the samurai were spent practicing unarmed martial arts, sword practice, and riding horses and shooting arrows. When they weren't practicing martial arts, they spent daily time in meditation and study. Some enjoyed writing or reciting poetry, the art of calligraphy, or flower arranging. The most fearsome warriors in history spent much time in very peaceful activities.

Facing page: A samurai reenactor in Japan dazzles a crowd with his archery skills. Real-life samurai practiced martial arts as well as more peaceful activities, such as poetry and calligraphy.

Above: A woman practices with a katana, often referred to as a samurai sword.

WOMEN

Most samurai were men, but there are a few examples of samurai women. Tomoe Gozen was a high-ranking officer in the Gempei War. She was renowned for her skill with the bow and arrow, and she could tame wild horses with ease. Ancient writings tell that when she fought with a sword, "she was a warrior worth a thousand."

Hangaku Gozen was another woman samurai. She was an expert archer, able to hit her target with pinpoint accuracy. One story has her defending a castle nearly single-handedly, but the enemy finally wounded her in both legs. The enemy took her prisoner, and then took her to the court of the enemy. According to one story, the enemy leader eventually fell in love with her and they were married.

In the history of Japan, women on the battlefield were the exception rather than the rule. However, many women trained with the *naginata*, a long pole with a blade on the end. Since many of them had to defend their homes while their husbands were at war, many women became experts with the naginata.

Below: A painting of a samurai in traditional official clothing.

CLOTHING

The samurai were always dressed appropriately for the occasion. They bathed frequently and took time for personal hygiene. They put lotion in their hair, and combed it back into a ponytail. People believed that a sloppy samurai was either drunk or a criminal.

In official duties, most samurai wore a very wide pair of pants called a *hakama*, and a jacket that had shoulders sticking out like a pair of wings.

Above: A samurai is served food and hospitality by two geishas, women who were trained to entertain with conversation, music, and dance.

LIVING QUARTERS

Before 1591, many samurai were farmers during peacetime. If there were no battles to fight or leaders to guard, they would go home to their farms and work the land. In 1591, however, the government forbade samurai from farming. After that, samurai lived near their *daimyo* (the local leader or lord of the area). Usually, they lived in barracks inside the city walls, inside the daimyo's castle. The samurai had few pieces of furniture within the house. The main room usually had one object—a painting, a scroll, or something that was intended to be thought-provoking.

FOOD

Samurai ate a wide variety of vegetables and seafood, but their main dish was rice. Rice could be cooked, ground into a paste, or mixed with vegetables. Because samurai were of a high social status, they generally ate better than the rest of the people. They typically ate brown rice. A treat while they were on the road was often a rice cake, dipped in honey or served with fruit. In addition to rice, they ate potatoes, radishes, cucumbers, beans, and other vegetables. They also ate many things from the ocean—from seaweed to fish to octopus. Over 50 different kinds of plants gave flavorings and spices to their food. Their main drink was tea. Sometimes they drank *sake* (pronounced "sock-ee"), an alcoholic drink made out of rice. During peacetime, many samurai enjoyed hunting, and ate duck, deer, and wild boar.

Below: Although the samurai ate a wide variety of food, their main dish was rice.

Armor and Weapons

Samurai wore elaborate pieces of armor to protect themselves during battle. Their armor was mainly composed of tiny pieces of metal, leather, and fabric sewn together, instead of one big piece of metal. The only place where the samurai wore a large, single piece of armor was around the neck, which helped to secure the helmet.

Below: A samurai warrior draws his sword, or katana.

Samurai wore armor on the chest and back, which formed a skirt. Large, broad pieces of armor protected the arms, and form-fitting armor wrapped around the lower legs. Samurai sometimes decorated their helmets with deer antlers, fake sword blades, or even golden horns.

The samurai trained with the bow and arrow. Their favorite use of the bow was shooting while riding a horse. They had to do a lot of practicing to shoot arrows while riding a galloping horse.

Many samurai also used spears, especially the lower-ranking warriors. Spears were cheaper to manufacture than swords. Also, a spear could be thrown. The naginata, a blade at the end of a long pole, was also a favorite of many samurai, since it was equally good on the ground, or fighting someone who was on a horse.

Samurai rarely carried shields. Their swords acted as a defensive weapon as well as an offensive weapon.

Guns were eventually introduced into Japan, but they were not in widespread use during the age of the samurai. Guns and gunpowder were very expensive, so not many people had access to them. The guns produced a huge amount of smoke, so after a few shots, no one could see anything on the battlefield. Also, the early guns were not very accurate, and the gunpowder might not fire in humid weather. Most samurai preferred the bow and arrow instead of guns. Arrows were more accurate, could be loaded faster, and could be reused. Guns became cheaper and more reliable in the 1800s, which is when samurai began to use them more.

Below: A ribbed samurai helmet decorated with golden deer antlers.

The Samurai Sword

The samurai's most important weapon, of course, was the sword. The samurai would never be without it, but it was bad manners to take it out so others could see it. The samurai would never show a common person the sword. If a high-ranking official asked to see the sword, the samurai would pull the sword out of its scabbard only a few inches. To take the sword completely out of its scabbard meant that there was going to be a fight, often to the death.

The samurai sword, called a *katana*, was a marvel of engineering. A master craftsman could take more than a month to make a sword. The craftsman would start by melting metal, even pots and pans. The heat of a specially made fireplace created molten metal, burning away the impurities. Then, the craftsman would pour the molten metal into the shape of a sword. While the metal was still warm, he would pound the sword with a hammer, flattening it out. He folded the metal over onto itself, and then cooled it in water. Then, he heated the sword up again, pounded it flat again, then folded it over. This hammering and folding, heating and cooling cycle was repeated dozens of times. It is what gave the samurai sword its legendary hardness and razor-sharp edge.

When the craftsman was satisfied with the sword, he began the polishing process. He first polished the sword with a pumice-like material, which smoothed the sword out. Then he polished it with a different material, which would remove the scratches left by the pumice. Twelve different materials were used, each one finer than the last. Each removed the scratches left by the previous material.

Below: A samurai helmet, wakizashi, and katana.

The twelfth material had the consistency of flour, which left the sword bright and shiny.

Finally, the craftsman would sign his name on the sword, underneath the handle. He then added the wooden handle and a decorative hand guard.

Ritual surrounded the making of a sword. There were certain foods the craftsman would not eat during the sword-making process. There were certain activities the craftsman would not do while making the sword. The making of the sword was a religious experience for the craftsman. The sword had religious significance for the samurai, too. The samurai called the sword "his soul," and it never left his side.

Typically, a samurai would carry two swords. The katana was usually a little more than three feet (.9 m) long. Samurai also carried a second sword, about two feet (.6 m) long, called a *wakizashi*. They would use the wakizashi if the katana broke, or for closer combat, or for the grim ritual of seppuku. Together, the two swords represented the high social status of the samurai.

The End of the Samurai

Shogun Toyotomi Hideyoshi unified the clans of Japan under a single ruler in the late 1500s. By the early 1600s, clan fighting over territory ended. With the end of the fighting, the samurai had no real purpose.

In the early 1600s, ambassadors from Asia and Europe wanted to meet with the leaders of Japan. However, the government feared that a local warlord would start to develop trade with other countries and become more powerful than the central government. Further, the shogun was afraid that some foreign visitors might be spies.

In 1641, Japan closed its doors. Strict limits were set on foreigners. No one could deal with them except the central government. The government also forbade samurai from leaving the country. Some foreign governments had been hiring samurai to fight in their military. The Japanese government, after 1641, forbade samurai from fighting for other countries.

Many of the samurai were bored. The government had forbidden them to farm or do any other work, but there was no work to do as samurai, either. As the economy grew, merchants and small business owners were making a good living. However, the samurai were on a fixed government salary. Some samurai had to give up their status in order to go to work to make enough money to survive.

Facing page: A full suit of samurai armor from the Tokyo Fuji Art Museum, in Tokyo, Japan.

Some samurai passed the time by dueling with other samurai. In 1650, the government passed a law that made it illegal for samurai to fight each other.

The skills of the samurai began to deteriorate. With no one to fight, they allowed themselves to lose the sharpness of their skills. Many quit practicing altogether. In 1690, the government actually had to pass a law requiring that samurai practice martial arts.

In 1853, warships from the United States came to Japan. With a show of the warships' destructive power, the Americans forced the Japanese to open their country to trade. This is an example of gunboat diplomacy—when a stronger country forces a weaker country into an agreement. The Americans forced Japan to sign a treaty.

Fearful that they had fallen behind in technology, the Japanese initiated immediate reforms to modernize their military, legal system, and schools. The shogunate government resigned, the feudal system ended, and the Japanese created a national army patterned after the armies of England and the United States. With a national army, there was no longer a need for samurai.

The final gasp of the samurai came in 1877, when the last few samurai rose up against the government, protesting the new reforms. Historians call this the *Satsuma rebellion*. It ended with the ritual suicide of their leader, a samurai named Saigo Takamori. Shortly thereafter, samurai lost the right to carry their swords. The age of the samurai had come to an end.

Facing page:
By the end of the nineteenth century, the samurai were obsolete. Their spirit, however, lives on.

GLOSSARY

Bushido

Bushido ("the way of the warrior") was a way of life, or personal code, held by Japanese samurai. Bushido emphasized loyalty, honor, and integrity.

Confederation

A loose collection of states or organizations united in an alliance. In early Japanese history, warlords ruled over many different clans, each with its own loyal armies, towns, and farms. In effect, Japan consisted of many small "countries." There were attempts over the years to unite these different clans into a single confederation. In the late 1500s, Toyotomi Hideyoshi finally succeeded in ruling over all the clans in a single Japanese confederation.

Daimyo

A ruler, or lord, of a clan or region. Daimyo pledged allegiance to the shogun.

Gunboat Diplomacy

Forcing a country into an agreement through the use of military might. In 1853, the United States sent warships to Japan to force that country to open its borders to trade.

Katana

A long, single-edged sword used by the samurai. Finely crafted, the katana had a slight curve, making it suitable for slashing attacks. Also called a samurai sword.

Oath

A serious promise to do something, or behave in a certain way. Samurai took an oath of loyalty to their leaders, and would fight to the death to protect them.

武 道

Ronin

Masterless samurai. This often happened because of a clan leader's death in battle. Ronin wandered the countryside, looking for work or offering their military services to the highest bidders. Sometimes ronin made money by dueling other samurai.

Seppuku

Ritual suicide performed by samurai when disgraced, especially after losing a battle. Also called *hara-kiri*.

Shogun

The military commander-in-chief of feudal Japan. Even though Japan had an emperor, the real power was held by the military.

Wakizashi

A smaller version of the katana. Both were carried by samurai. The wakizashi was useful for close combat, and for the grim ritual of seppuku.

Left: Kendo is a sport that has its roots in the samurai art of swordsmanship. Competitors use bamboo swords and heavy padding for protection. Kendo is practiced by millions of people worldwide.

INDEX